medical degree from the University of Santo Tomas. Her residency training led her to Harlem Hospital, Rochester General Hospital, and a the University of Texas in San Antonio, including her fellowship in the same institution. She is a diplomate in Obstetrics/Gynecology and has been in private medical practice for more than three decades.

Dr. Mayuga comes from an illustrious family. Both parents, Dr. Joaquin Cartagena, a pioneering physician, and Rosario Vendivil, a pharmacist and leading educator, were political and public figures. She is the youngest of five siblings.

Having lived through the remnants of the Second World War, some of the episodes in her book, **Immigrant at Peace - A Woman Physician Reflects**, published in 1997, bear her impressions and experiences. As a medical physician in training at the heart of the civil rights struggle, her medical odyssey has spanned a 34-year period, culminating in her private practice in Pasco, Washington. She is the first Filipino OB-GYN specialist practitioner in the state of Washington. She is published in six poetry anthologies in the US and is currently working on her third prose and poetry book, this one on politics and other social issues.

Dr. Mayuga is an active civic, cultural, and religious leader who works with total dedication and with a sense of mission. She has written essays, critiques, and observations on social and political topics, including issues on health care. She has two children, a physician and an educator, and is married to Dr. Simeon Mayuga. They live in Pasco, Washington. You may write to her at 531 W. Park, Suite #1, Pasco, Washington, 99301.

Spring, Autumn, Sunset

a collection of inspirational
and compassionate poetry

from the author of *Immigrant at Peace*
Enriqueta Cartagena Mayuga, M.D.

Edited by Tanya Sorenson

BLACK FOREST PRESS
San Diego, California
December, 2000
First Edition

Dr. Simeon S. Mayuga
5306 W. Irving St.
Pasco, WA 99301-3004

Spring, Autumn, Sunset

*a collection of inspirational
and compassionate poetry*

from the author of Immigrant at Peace
Enriqueta Cartagena Mayuga, M.D.
Edited by Tanya Sorenson

PUBLISHED IN THE UNITED STATES OF AMERICA
BY
BLACK FOREST PRESS
P.O.Box 6342
Chula Vista, CA 91909-6342
1-800-451-9404

Cover design by
Dale and Penni Neely

Disclaimer

This document is an original work of the author. It may include reference to information commonly known or freely available to the general public. Any resemblance to other published information is purely coincidental. The author has in no way attempted to use material not of her own origination. Black Forest Press disclaims any association with or responsibility for the ideas, opinions or facts as expressed by the author of this book.

Printed in the United States of America
Library of Congress
Cataloging-in-Publication

ISBN: 1-58275-054-8
Copyright © December, 2000 by Enriqueta Cartagena Mayuga
ALL RIGHTS RESERVED

Table of Contents

Acknowledgement
Dedication
Foreword i
Introduction vii
Always the Spirit Flows.................................... 1
Winner at Last: Grand Slam of the Soul 3
I Will Dwell in the House of the Lord 5
The Contrite's Story - Peace in Silence.................. 9
Life's Performance 11
Tarhata 13
Last Night's Dream - Life's Synergy..................... 15
No More Ace to Play..................................... 17
The Misfit - Prodigal Child 19
Closure 21
Invoking His Grace...................................... 23
Alive and Kicking - Am Still in the Running............. 25
Believe - For Your Faith Will Set You Free 27
I Gave it My Best Shot 31
Not the Meekest Lamb.................................... 34
A Victim No More.. 35
In His Shoes 37
Missteps and the Superman............................... 39
Life Is Beautiful 40
Never Too Late 42
No Longer In Fear....................................... 44
Spring, Autumn, Sunset.................................. 46
The Psalm of the Prodigal Son 48
The Second Fiddle 50
The Saga of the Penitent................................ 52
Too Late to Matter...................................... 55
Rolando 56
No Way Out 59

There is Still Time...60
I "Done" It All..62
Too Soon 64
Act of Contrition 66
Past My Prime..68
God's Day - First Day of Spring 71
It Is About Time 72
What Follows Next 74
For We Have Just Begun 78
The Ascent - By a Mountain Climber of Life 79
Let the Day Begin 81

Acknowledgements

To Gail Vanderschoor - friend, nurse-turned-transcriptionist, advisor, an artist herself who tediously "deciphered" my penmanship (more like hieroglyphics).

To Willie Zaragoza - who wrote the original bio (my first book "Immigrant at Peace") upon which the amended version is based.

To Dahk Knox, Ph.D., my publisher, and his staff: Keith Pearson, Production Manager; Elizabeth Farrell, Copy Editor; Inga Gleason, Project Manager; and Jodi Mabry, Press Manager.

To Carissa Irog - computer whiz, part time transcriptionist, "Girl Friday."

I am grateful for the support and prayers of my husband, Simeon, children: Lorena and Enrico.

I appreciate the "readers and listeners" La Donna Volmer, Dr. Shireen Mahsud, Irene Torres, Roxanne Wokojance, and others who facilitated the process: Gloria Cartagena Go, Cherry Safford, Luz Tuazon, Julie Vanderschoor, and many wonderful friends and supporters.

I am deeply grateful to Father Skok of Spokane, Washington and to Jean hall of New Mexico, Sylvia Mayuga of Manila for their precious time and expertise in kindly sharing this poetic journey with me.

I reserve a very special place for my dedicated editor and friend, Tanya Sorenson who set the goal for me a year ago to write these poems and bring it to completion. Her faith in my literary quest and the refinement she inspired in my writing is invaluable and immeasurable.

Dedication

To Simeon, my beloved husband:
    The passage was narrow
    but the coast is clear

To my grandchildren
    Sofia Simone and Isabella Rose:
    Sometime soon —
    it will be harvest time.

To Tanya Sorenson
    Editor, friend, exemplary human being
    – I am forever grateful.

Foreword

I.

"Medical doctor" conjures up images of office white coats, surgical baggy green smocks and pants, carefully excised biopsies, deft surgical strokes, neatly sutured wounds, scientific diagnosis, and frightening or reassuring prognosis. There is much the image of the detached scientist and cold professional.

Dr. Mayuga's collection of poetry, **Spring, Autumn, Sunset,** belies the image of the *professional* medical professional. It probes beneath the organic tissue of the human person to find the spirit and, like X-rays, expose the soul.

Our lives can be caught up in a world of the technical jargon of cyberspace and the fastest means to access it. We can become engrossed in the business world of the unyielding fiscal calculations marking the ups and downs of the Wall street dream. We fend off the bombardment of extravagant advertising claims. We bear the deadening, repetitive television routine of situation comedies and game shows — even those which promise a million dollars to the masters of trivia. In the daily menu of newspapers and the weekly or monthly fare of journals, we suffer a prose of atrophied vocabulary, unimaginative ill-constructed sentences, and spin-doctored paragraphs of half-truths.

The poet, even the medical doctor poet, anomalous as that may sound, provides a welcome, inspiring relief. The poet, in the Greek sense, is a *maker.* The poet, in the English sense, is a *seer* (see-er). The poet does not so much search out the beauty of things but the truth of things. That is why poets are always dangerous. By the arrangement of chosen words, the poet brings to the surface of consciousness experiences, ideas, and emotions, and **makes** them powerful in concentrated, imaginative speech. The poet takes seemingly ordinary and routine experiences and **sees** the truth that lies beneath. The poet, in clear vision, peels of the surface and unmasks the reality. That is why the poet is dangerous. The poet can terrorize the complacent, self-satisfied, consumer-sated mind.

That is what Dr. Mayuga does in her volume, ***Spring, Autumn, Sunset.*** Her poems are earthy, perhaps far more earthy than she realizes. At times her poems are whimsical. But always they are deeply spiritual. They reveal her inner person, which provides a window for us to see more clearly our own inner person.

Do I have favorites? "Spring, Autumn, Sunset" touched me first. "Past My Prime," "Never Too Late," and "Life's Performance" spoke to this aging theology professor. But each poem did for me what poetry is supposed to do: offer a vision which uplifts, inspires, entertains, and challenges. Poetry helps us to see better and to do better. That is what her collection of poems did for me.

Dr. Mayuga's life is not an ordinary life. There are many stories, both ordinary and exotic, which she can and does tell. They tease our minds as they open us up to her world. Her poetry is a succinct, delightful shortcut into that world — and into her soul and our souls as well.

Charles D. Skok, Doctor of Theology (STD),
Doctor of Law (honoris causa),
Professor Emeritus of Religious Studies
Gonzaga University

II.

"Whoever wears not the Sampaguita is no Filipina," wrote the distinguished Filipino poet, Manuel Bernabe. "Sampaguita" and "Filipina" — simple words, but the meanings they symbolize are emotionally provoking to the natives of the Philippines. The meaning of Sampaguita is "sumpa kita" (I, or we, pledge), which symbolizes the central theme of this book: Dr. Enriqueta Mayuga struggles to accomplish her youthful pledge, dreams and aspirations. Passionately expressed, at times objectively critical, other times subjectively despondent, her poems give tone and texture to the dream where "one day the fish of the sea and the birds of the air will get together with men of all races, colors and creeds; even the deprived would sing songs of contentment and remember that one woman did make a difference" (***Immigrant at Peace***, Mayuga, 1997).

Poetry, her choice of medium to express these sentiments, is the favored expression of a true Filipino. Songs, myths, legends, and poetry have been preserved orally among Filipinos since ancient times. In the 19th century, "balagtasan," the art of poetical joust, was frequently performed as social entertainment. Poetry has been the medium of choice for heroes of the Philippines. The famous poem "My Last Farewell," was written by Dr. Jose Rizal, our national hero, the night before his execution. He, too, was a medical doctor. Thus, from ancient times, Filipinos have been keenly tuned to the inherent powers of words, especially when used in poetry, to express emotions, share knowledge, and enhance enlightenment.

Like Rizal, Mayuga's love for poetry was inspired by her mother. Now a mother herself, as well as a wife, a medical doctor, a writer, and a poet, she has the youth in mind, where she hopes to make a difference.

The sentiments expressed, including the bitterness, can be poignantly appreciated from a cultural orientation. As an educated young Filipina, her dream of "making a difference" is consistent with the Philippine society's expectation for a bright promising star. Since early times, a Filipina has been seen as economically, politically, and socially equal to a male. "Once an artist, a prodigy ("A Victim - No More") and "Never the compliant, always the rebel — the innovator, the pioneer, the trail blazer" ("No More Ace to Play") are the words she uses to describe herself. Mayuga's undaunted courage in facing immense obstacles is vividly expressed: "I swam haphazardly against unspeakable tides; I scaled steep cliffs with edges scarred; I implored the heavens, my lofty dreams" ("I Gave It My Best Shot"). But her dream "to make a difference" should not by any means be misconstrued as self-seeking, nor be associated with motives of self-aggrandizement. Her motives are laudable and consistent with her cultural beliefs. Reared in an upper-class environment with opportunities to achieve an advanced education and to acquire accolades for her achievements, she "was reared to save the world — to correct its inequities" ("Alive and Kicking — Am Still in the Running"). Given these opportunities and consequent achievements, she was expected to give back to the society that nurtured her growth so that she might fulfill her "utang na loob" (debt of honor). Her chosen profession in the medical field and her dreams to be the "innovator, the pioneer, and the trail blazer" are repayment manifestations of this debt of honor. And in healing people, like a true Filipina, she exercises the "bayanihan" (cooperative) virtue of helping others.

Emigrating to this country nearly four decades ago, she would face the formidable challenges of all professional women in America during the tumultuous period of the 1960s, plus those of a minority. She finds that in America the world equality is elusive. As a healer, she would be subjected to "acid tongue and racial slurs. . . relegated to a lesser role, irrelevant I am" ("The Second Fiddle"). But her genuine pride as a Filipina has sustained her through her challenges and endeavors, and has proven her to be as durable as the native "narra" tree and as resilient as bamboo. And true to her underlying spiritual faith, she's determined to "reach the mountain peak and set the anchor tight" for she believes "in this ascent" and "in the faith that empowers" her ("The Ascent - By the Mountain Climber of Life).

There is much food for thought in this outpouring of passionate and honest emotions of one immigrant who has had to prove herself invincible as a woman and as a doctor. And in sharing her courageous bouts, she ultimately offers hope, bearing the gift of faith and revealing that strong character that Filipinos so much admire. By writing about her experiences and making them known to others, she has become the trailblazer of her dreams, and a role model for those who follow.

A lei of Sampaguita would look exquisite around her neck, and its wondrous fragrance would soothe the souls of others she comes in contact with wherever she goes. For she is truly a remarkable Filipina!

Jean Quintero Hall
Faculty, Western New Mexico University
Rizal and Philippines History Scholar
Author, poet, newspaper columnist

III.

My long-lost and recently found relative Enriqueta Cartagena-Mayuga is something of a phenomenon in an age of globalization. To begin with, she is a doctor who is also a poet casting an anguished eye of empathy at the wounded. This would make her unique enough on our native soil, the Philippines, where great need often dulls a physician's sensitivity to the great need of so many. In hi-tech America, my Manang Rikki is a walking protest placard at the impersonal culture of mainstream medicine in the world's wealthiest country.

Her poetry and the earlier essays that percolated through three decades as an immigrant female physician in America before bursting into the world are the progress report of a soul's divine unease. Beneath the activist sentiments beats the childhood faith of a little hometown girl still struggling to defend the deepest things she knows in a strange land where she has passionately sought to make a difference.

"The drama of the self-unfolding is greater than the drama of nations," once wrote a fellow-poet, Anais Nin. This could not be truer of Enriqueta Cartagena-Mayuga as she travels her immigrant years in retrospect, taking the measure of her success and failure in the deepest language of the soul. Old enough now to do so with an unblinking eye, she admits shortcomings as she celebrates quiet victories, harvesting hope for us all.

Sylvia L. Mayuga
Manila, Sept.11, 2000
Filipino Poet, Author,
Journalist, Environmentalist
Palanca Award recipient
Fulbright-Hayes scholar

Introduction

Several years ago, a woman called me, explaining that she wrote in her spare time and wondered if I would look at the pieces. Little did I know that Dr. Enriqueta Cartagena Mayuga's desire to capture for her progeny over 30 years of her writings, penned in delivery rooms and hospital breezeways, would lead to such a wonderful, blessed adventure. Working with Dr. Mayuga has been a gift in my life. We put together her first book, *Immigrant at Peace*, as a legacy. But her incredible talent has more to offer, as the success of her first work showed. She sees her world, and the world of women of color, women of non-American origin, women of passion and politics in ways that enlighten and inspire.

As a child, she grew up passionately involved in politics, for instance, being junior mayor for two weeks. As an adult, her keen mind has continually quested for political truth, for ethics, for morality in our ever-changing culture. And through it all, her faith has never wavered, serving to strengthen her through many adversities.

She has found her voice in her writings, and they are truly a gift to this world. I submit this volume with gratitude for the love she has shown me, with awe at the talent that seems endless, and with devotion to letting others hear themselves in her voice.

Tanya Sorenson, M.Ed.
Kent, Washington
September 4, 2000

Always the Spirit Flows

Be good to me
for I will not always be here for you.
Fate has its own perfidious moods
like the tropics has its monsoons.
Nothing in life is certain –
even the logical does not follow.

Nothing is truly predictable
even the rational.
In a moment, I can be drawn by the West wind
never to return –
Sucked by the quicksand of life
into an impenetrable clutch,
never to resurface.

In a moment, the murky water of life and its pollutants
can choke me into oblivion.
At any time, each of use has
a sword of Damocles to fear,
an awaiting flood,
an earthquake lurking –
crumbling and cracking our very
foundation.

In a moment, life can be snuffed out
like a petal,
like feathers plucked,
like dust blown and displaced.
But life is not only inane
nor insane.

It is a dichotomy I present to you –
not to be fatalistic,
But to be contemplative,
not to be hopeless,
But to be open for adversity.
To allow the spirit to take hold,
to sprout its buds, spread its wings,
Men come and go.

I might be gone for you –
but always
The Spirit flows.

Winner at Last : The Grand Slam of the Soul

Never the winner, never the bride,
I go through life philosophically.
One time a princess, never the Queen,
My fortune has slipped so woefully,
Away from the accolades of the throngs,
Away from the path to the throne.

Victory has slipped from my wrinkled hands,
The crown is all but lost,
Yet I know too well with hope serene,
I could still deter the machine –
Fate's machine which has denied –
My medal, my trophy, my feminine pride.

The presidency in truth has eluded me,
The CEO job was not to be,
But the process is there waiting for me,
If I reject a life of ignominy,
If I could only see the best in me,
Then losing is but a formality.

At sixty one, I must believe,
Serendipity still exists,
I must stay on through the course –
For giving up is much, much worse,
True, I have not obtained my MVP,
But a Michael Jordan is a rarity.

We are not truly captains of our souls,
There are other ways to triumph deep,
I may not have won the championship,
But I have gained more in His kind hands,
A rested soul, a life serene,
My Grand Slam from God's great machine.

I Will Dwell in the House of the Lord

"I will dwell in the house of the Lord," said he.
How about man in our time?
Where does he dwell?
What does he say?

"Millennium is coming!"
Everyone pauses in anticipation
The coming Y2K
"Beware of the computer glitch!"
Tons of warning, floating papers
inundate us.
"Hold onto your records," we are told.
"Store beef, sardines, dried fruits, canned vegetables."
We need all these for eventuality –
backup generator, flashlight,
kerosene lamps, and all.

Man actually resides in his own world –
in his very own home
These caves of darkness, of anxieties,
These caverns of dysfunctionalities,
Passion repressed by societal norms
yet even when free, we are not truly free.
For in rebelling against society's norms –
men focus on a dual confusion:
to what is right as well as
to what is farcical.

He holds on to his very own version –
"Give to Caesar what's Caesar's"
"Give to God what's God's,"
– as long as it fits Man's scheme.
Pride chases men – chases all of us –
through our enclaves,
in the ghetto of our souls,
in our corporate offices,
in our schools,
in our places of worship.

Like Machiavelli
we have our own hidden agenda –
with Freudian aspects
that glamorize our ego.
"Free choice," we call it,
actually, well-crafted rebellion
with legalities covered:
"When it looks good – it is right."
"When I feel good – it is good."
"Whatever works for me is what counts."

Indeed, we have invented our own God –
"It is legal – so what's wrong?"
Morality? Who invented it?
Man's contraption he debunks,
Manipulation and stonewalling, double-talk
are the rules of the day.

Out from heaven, from the Mount –
He sees and shakes His head.

From the Valley of Death
From the Purgatory of wanton souls
Mammon awaits in glee!
"See what free choice does to man –
languishing in chains
but he does not know it!"

"The time of reckoning is so distant,
there is enough time left for
sinning and experimenting,
inflicting pain,
fussing and amending norms."
In Limbo – he lives,
In Limbo – he dies!

But men recognize not Satan's scheme –
Man hears not the message from the stable,
hears not his sermon from the Mount,
declining the musing of His Spirit.

Man misses the point – Big time!
The biggest point of all:
His Magnificent masterpiece,
God's spectacular creation –
The Messianic Mystics – of the biological scheme
the interplay of X and Y,
the blastocyst which follows,
finally the embryo of life itself!

As a man of science – he is aware. . .
of atoms, molecules,
translocation, nuclear fission,
contraceptions,
But to him, oocyte and blastocyst
are just cellular events –
in a cow,
a plant,
More complex than the amoebae.

In his own Citadel –
he equates Humans –
to Cheetah:
"So where's the beef?"
– the existentialists say.

"I will dwell in the House of the Lord" –
"In the Valley of Death I fear no evil,
for thou art with me."

Past the Millennium –
Past the Quintenium –

Man Beware. . . .

The Contrite's Story - Peace in Silence

All my life, I have wailed and whined –
    and this has never hurt me,
Undeterred by protesting friends,
I go through life neurotically.

But alas one day, I found it hard,
    to see all my loved ones gone,
To their earthly home – the peace they crave,
    to the total silence of their grave.

If I could change the present tide,
    reshape my life, accept the world,
I would gift my friends with loving glance –
    and silent tears to their heart's content.

Valid may be my claim to pain,
Still no word will suffice –
    to soothe my aches, my angry soul,
For earth is hell, not paradise.

Now I realize that words could hurt –
    even those with battle scars,
Men's imperfections will never end –
    and verbal excess is life's torment.

Today I resolve to make amends,
        to my family, my deceased friends,
I will look at heaven with contrition,
I will look forward to God's rendition.

I will forget my pains and forgive my friends,
My lips will forever be sealed,
In memory of loved ones killed
        by verbal abuse — gone to their silent graves.

Beyond the clouds - the blue sky reigns,
In this human earth, some things are true,
No man, no word could ever correct,
Faults that only God can alone perfect.

Life's Performance

We form alliances, then we regroup,
We dispense forgiveness and ask for mercy ourselves,
We fine tune our thoughts to realign the mechanics of life,
We overhaul our engine and recharge our battery,
We strengthen our physique and master our emotions,
We keep groping for the right words and
adapting different stance,
We follow the ABC's of our earlier nurturing –
even as we tinker, modify, and recreate.

At times we have done better than our forbearers –
a few times we have far outpaced them.
Many times just to be at par with our elders or
our peers would suffice;
A few times we seem never to get it, never to win it.
Sometimes the prize seems to be within our grasp:
the promised land is at hand.
We climb and clamber only to fall, and without
hesitation we try again still only to come out with the
same results.
By sheer persistence somehow we could negotiate
ourselves out of a quandary –
and escape the bruising quagmire – but Oh! – so
much trauma,
so much fracture, and the permanent concussion of our
souls.

Without our engine being rechecked or our wheel
being aligned
we are apt to go back again and again
through the same ruinous paths
with the same old results.

Unless we allow ourselves to be greased by the oil
of the basics
and allow the Spirit to take over,
Unless we allow the angels to navigate us through
the deep waters,
shedding off the chemical and emotional abuse –
We won't be able to start the engine of life or
keep the motor running.

TARHATA*

I have seen your high, I have seen your low,
I helped you glide through waves of doom,
I have seen you past the tyrant's jaw,
His savage sweep of lives in throe,
Imprisoned soul thou child of gloom,
A remorseful earth deprived of bloom.

I admire forever your strength –
Not your raging flesh – your carnal scar,
I implored your piety to no avail,
Sadly Mammon's powers have prevailed.
My love for you does not allow,
The dancing dervish to rule the mind,
The God in me refuses to abide –
To cruel fate – where dreams to die.

At times I would sink to despondency,
Unable to accept your destiny,
Cocaine consigning you to ignominy,
My stubborn heart cannot accept –
    the naked truth, divine regret,
Your drowning in the sea of murk,
The fervid sun and weeping wind –
Awakens me – this hopeless dream.

If I could turn back the hands of time,
To disown the present, to revive the dream,
If I could pluck the arrow, dart, and sting,
Rejoin the seams of your disjointed heart.
If I could pick the debris, your base defunct,
Glue tight your pieces – my magic wand,
If I could expose that tiger's lair,
Debone the shark, level the pride,
If I could turn the fox in each of us,
Reducing it into a loving lamb,
    Then I could open heaven's pearly gate,
    To paradise, where love is done.

*a beautiful Moslem name in southern Philippines

Last Night's Dream - Life's Synergy

You awake me from my ethereal silence,
    from the dreams you have created for me.
In a vignette –
    you glide, you float, you clamber –
        dancing in your struggles with copious
            sweat and tears.

Searching through the impenetrable clouds –
    Through my opaque body,
        still believing in a fulfilling world to come –
    your eyes more subdued,
    the dynamics of virtue in retreat,
     your spirit half surrendering,
     my mind dazed to an optimism half gone.
I thought of your dreams –
    illusions, fantasies, air castles –
        whirling and berating
            my sighing soul.

Helpless from afar –
    memories surge through my tenuous veins
    trying to attain some sense of contentment.
In my semi-arid plane of existence, I want to return –
    to retrace once more
    my sleep pathway,
        where my mind is dulled,
            disallowing illusions
        that drown me.

I wish to go —
    where time is at a standstill,
        where no one prods,
            and no one probes,
My agitated soul left in peace —
    left to explore my God.

His grace needed to make me understand,
    he fusion of reality to my destiny —
        the merger of energy to wisdom
            —the synergy of the soul and the spirit.

No More Ace to Play

Never the princess,
    always the Queen,
Never the bridesmaid,
    always the bride,
Never timid,
    always assertive,
Never a follower,
    always a leader,
Never the compliant,
    always the rebel –
        the innovator, the pioneer, the trail blazer.
Never a listener,
    always the story teller,
Never a giver,
    always the taker,
Never the frightened,
    always the fearless,
Never the cautious,
    always the impudent,
Never the water,
    always the fire,
    the flame, the blaze, the tempest.

–Yet my world appears incomplete,
I am a take charge person –
    or so I thought!

I profess being in control –
> but of what
> and of whom?
Repeatedly I declared,
> "I am the master of my fate"
>> – but could it be this desolate?

I should have been a clown –
> for all the world to laugh,
> a victim – for me to empathize,
> a slave – groveling on my knee
>> so I could reach your heart.

Could it be that I should be content
> as a supporting cast –
> not the heroine, who wins the Tenor of life?
Perhaps I should be bereft
> of men's passion for self-gratification
> be free from contrived comforts
>> and their lustful directions,
Where at last my soul – stark naked –
> would open to His call,
> where there is no more Ace to play –
And the only triumph, the only victory,
> is the peace and joy within.

The Misfit – Prodigal Child

Always the outsider, always the misfit,
I trek through life uninhibitedly,
Never the conformist, never compliant,
I faced society with defiance,
Attracted I was to alien call,
Always doubting the Holy Scroll.

Years of searching for my niche,
Years of pondering where I belong,
Not sure if I will ever find my own
    Place in the sun, in this mire,
      My role in this planetary quagmire.

A constant struggle to be myself,
A relentless pursuit to fate unknown,
A painful search to find a home,
A pathetic cry to the great beyond,
A petulant life, I tried to live,
Always the victim, always in need.

I tried to connect with social norms,
I found myself not being me,
I tried my best to compromise,
I wore make-up, the proper attire,
Singing the appropriate songs,
Waltzing on my queenly throne.

The perfume "My Sin", was appropriate,
To attract the glitz, Hollywood's bait,
My music was rock and roll,
And rock I did on this earthly shore,
My tango steps, I now bemoan,
The march of life, I should have known.

As I grew old, I realized,
My steps were wrong, I needed advice,
For God can see the truth that's lost,
When vainly I danced with my earthly toes,
Mistakes I once haughtily proclaimed,
My soul now contrite, with inner shame.

At 61, I feel secure,
Within His grasp, I have matured,
No more torment, no more pretense,
To men's madness, slave no more,
The divine in me has erased the plaques,
One time applied by social maps.

Now, I am free for the world to see,
My chains are all but gone,
Jigsaw puzzles, phantom masks,
None will deter me – my Christian task,
Today, I see the Promised Land,
    At last I feel my God at hand.

Closure

I am past the pain, the hurt, the inebriation,
    past the ire, the rancor, the intoxication,
    past rummaging through my eclectic values,
For life is more than just a toxic well gone dry,
    more than just the spiraling of birds –
    not merely the unmasking of men's dark side –
        their satanic claims,
It is also a revelation of men's goodness and greatness,
        the just jubilation of the eternal spring.

I am past dodging the waves to self-inflict,
    past the savage quest to unseat
    vulgar men and their worthless needs.
I am past the ferocious jaws of disgrace,
    past the threatening carnal vibes,
    past the mirage which choked each dream,
    past land mines, quicksand which sucks me in
        – to my beaten path,
        where I strayed – my fun-filled years,
        where naive virtues embraced the thorn,
          – entangled in its chaotic forms.

I am past the dreary tunnel on the track,
    – the hidden caves of endless wait – unrequited love,
    hard work unrewarded, loyalty uncompensated,
    justice in abeyance, hopes unanswered,

past the dying inferno of unbridled passion,
past the chasm of endless nights,
past the claws of the human flesh —
    of honor lost,
past the fire, the goal, the dream,
    in vain searching for one just man,
    awaiting His verdict,
        His judgment near,
        His mercy,
            my cross to bear.

Invoking His Grace

Lord – let me exalt you,
      usher me to the wonder of your love,
Spur me to seek redress
      – only from you
      – in your celestial fire,
Banish my cosmic fancies
    my ephemeral link
Let me waft through this turbulence
      – the unsettling limbo where I tread
Let me engage only in the noble cause:
    the total immersion of my soul to yours,
Pour me your sanctifying grace
   splashing the celestial condiment,
Curb my inexorable appetite –
    for the trite and temporal,
Free me from this chaotic flood
     – the cascading galaxies of earthly lure
     – the predatory lust
   which have imprisoned me in my
   nascent years,
Destroy the magic, the mesmeric hold
     the avarice in each of us,
Let me yearn only for the gleaming
    silvery stream which purifies the soul

Let the beaming sunlight
    radiate your clarity
        – and melt our fragile flesh,
Let your music vibe with resonance
    to an unlistening humanity
Grant me true peace
    the ethereal, I must yearn
For I could only try
    but nimble is my resolve
Without your illuminating grace.

Alive and Kicking – Am Still in the Running

I am no longer relevant,
    I am just an artifact,
    Once a giant of many talents
        an iridescent mind, a voluptuous face,
        a promising star – to carry the nation's flag,
    Once the mother of hope, to lead a change
        – centuries of impaired colonial thoughts,
        – victims of atrocious oppressors,
        – resigned and consigned
            to being second class.
I was the child groomed to make a difference
    – who will decimate the world's ills,
        its poverty, godlessness, emptiness,
    – the one who would break the socio-cultural
        schizophrenia of the conquered
    – the one who would foment only noble thoughts,
        an idealized state,
I was reared to save the world – to correct its iniquities,
        to spice and splice it with the sacred honey,
        A perennial bloom with its hypnotic spell,
        I was the embodiment of a solid youth –
            incisive mind, athletic prowess
            a graceful spirit – limitless horizon.
Now in my declining years –
    I still have the panache,
        vestigial hopes, exciting moments –

– but only for a short while,
– only after a good night's sleep,
– only after the masseur is finished working
    on my sore joints, my tight muscles.
My thoughts are not archaic –
  I am still contemporaneous
    but no longer do I excite the youth,
Gone is the public acclamation –
    Gone is the superior commendation –
      the adoring fans,
My children now think I am neat –
    more like a past icon, though,
But make note – I have not given up....
  I intend to make my presence known –
    to my daughter – now refocused
    to kinship,
    to my son, now less confused
      who once thought I was a clown
      but now I am to him
        a clown philosopher.

After all, the public revels on the titillating tales
    and double talk from the highest office –
Why should my genuine cry, my altruistic ideals
  be ignored?

I refused to be a relic, a footnote of history,
  a hostage to a memory,
  Listen! I am alive and kicking
  I am still in the running,
  For you ain't seen nothing yet!

Believe -
For Your Faith Will Set You Free

How do I fit in my new abode –
    past quagmire unresolved,
    the broken tendrils of youth gone by
    past my forsaken place
        in no man's land.

How do I indulge in the feast of life
    minus its excesses,
    the tempting lure of appetite,
        filling my barren flesh.
How do I break the hypnotic spell
    of an alluring world
    and emerge free
        from my captive's nest.
How would I subdue the cruel blow
    of unruly fate –
    these vicissitudes of life,
    the haunting maelstrom –
        my timorous flight.

How often can I stand up after each fall
    – to rebound after each break
    my life in constant upheaval,
    battling for a place in this,
        my unholy land.
How long should I go on musing vainlessly
for my love's return

– detach myself from my nihilistic world
– disengage from the unbridled fire
which fury lashes wantonly
at my shell of ice.

Can I ever go back –
to reenter the womb of life –
the maternal carriage
that nurtured me in my troubled waters,
seeking once more to be re-born
to be recycled
– to be re-invented
away from this cosmic world.
Will I ever be done to perfection –
where my wound would be effaced –
and no signs of prior scars
will mar my face.
How could I exalt in victory
amidst the debris –
the river of hopeless lives
inflamed minds
bleeding hearts.
Can I return in time –
to rebound, to recreate,
to remake myself –
yielding to no one that is farcical,
given another chance,

another role, another aria,
    in a new stage —
        another dais.

    Will I be able to pick up the broken jar —
to retrieve the piece
    to glaze, to fuse,
        to reattach them together like one —
        and be whole again.
Will I be able to bury my youth misspent
    — the countless seeds of ignorance
    — deplorable thoughts
    — despicable pride.
When will this end — my peripatetic ways,
    festooned with dark curiosities,
    evincing fear after each rejection —
        this emotional conundrum.
As God listens, the angels sing:
    "Believe, have faith —
        for your faith will set you free,
From the dissonance of your soul,
    its asynchronic ways,
Believe in the sublime
    in lives reborn
    in the Divine Spectacle
        of forgiveness and salvation.

Let the pain egress this very moment,
    let the fervid rays of the Spirit
        flow –
shimmering through your opaque
    soul
allowing His Kingdom to prevail.

And the sun peacefully rises,
    As hope rebounds
        A new soul is gently re-born.

I Gave It My Best Shot

I gave it my best shot — I gave you my all,
 I swam haphazardly against unspeakable tide,
 I scaled steep cliffs with edges scarred,
 I implored the heavens, my lofty dreams,
 I kiss the ground you treaded on
  — a ground void of topsoil nutrient sweet,
  — a ground of sand and rock
   with its soul and essence lost.
On my knees, I crawled
 I stifled my wants,
Prepared a path for your coming home
 from your capricious ways
  — erratic steps
  — our pagan quest,
Long hours with interminable angst,
Vying for unjustified fate, hoping you'd realize
 that you defied the rules of the game
 that you didn't play square
  — enroute to shame,
Casting your lot in the devil's lair,
Casting darkness to my once luminous world,
Unnerving a life, my planetary space,
 where once you were my sanctuary.
Once I pined for you who discovered me,
 The first good man, the last good man
  in my solitary nest
   — or so I thought,

Early in my youth you came to me
    – the primary icon of my troubled quest,
Exquisite and magnificent you were –
    with wit and masculine bearing beyond compare,
A promising seed from a cosmic God,
My long awaited Nirvana
    of an unworthy earth.

Now, no longer are our bodies one,
    lives once fused, bones once joined,
Emotions once unscripted,
    now fractured,
        dismantled,
            dislocated.
His mind once keen and robust
    now irretrievably reduced to dust and smog.
Where once I was weak, frightened and frayed,
    Now I have found my elusive peace.

As I finally respond to God's gracious call
    casting aside my impious ways,
        spurning the chaotic ghetto of my soul,
Away from the man I adored,
    way from the man who turned
        not to be –
            the fidelity of my life.

As life's unremitting shadows fall,
    I look back at the good, the bad,
        and the beautiful –
Indeed, I did give it my best shot –
    warts and all!
No blaming, no brooding,
    no fussing, no fuming,
Call it pilot's error of my maiden flight
    in this cosmic earth,
        this aerospace of human life,
Now past my human idolatry,
Now past forsaking the intangibles,
    past forsaking the soul's neurons,
Finally paying homage to my waiting God,
    the true Nirvana –
        my celestial Dawn.

Not the Meekest Lamb

I may not be the meekest lamb
    or the most pliant pet –
But I carry with me the longevity
    of wisdom of years,
I may not be a penthouse
    harboring the magnificent view
        or salivating in the comfort of the rich –
But I harbor prudence
    knowing my priority – focused on my goals,
At times I may be accused of temerity
But mistake it not for impetuousness
    for I do not carry the harshness of the
        proud,
Even the Son of God humbly knelt
    to wash men's feet,
        – was crucified so men might live
        and know His might
Clearly He has set the tone for me –
Bold or meek as you may perceive me to be
I have made the best of choices:
    A lust for peace
    A life of love
Simply, I am proud to be His.

A Victim - No More

Go away, my mind is clear,
    I am not your willing prey,
No longer will I forfeit
    my new life of resolve,
        – away from the avarice,
            the lust, the drugs,
        – away from the hedonistic god
            of contemporaneous men.
In perpetual Limbo I was,
    – the Earthly purgatory of the corrupt,
    – with brazen defilement of His truth,
    – favoring prurient life –
        an errant life that is now passé,
Subject no more to your scheming heart,
    – free from the gridlock of my past,
        surrendering to the comfort of you flesh
            – the vicarious life I chose to lead.
Too long drowned in this dichotomy
    – between the right and wrong,
    – between the trite and worthwhile,
    choked by the vile and vengeful dust,

No more barrier to my path:
    the joyful renewal of my soul,
With you, I was decerebrate,
    my mind mirrored my incontinent soul,
Once an artist, a prodigy,

– now a broken lyre,
– discordant note
– a national voice.

Today at last I am free,
my disabling ways, my hostile past,
I need no yeoman to save my soul,
for with God, I can fend off foes
– the poison dart, the jagged knife,
no more intrusion in my new sojourn
Within His wings – my new life of peace,
Within His love I am secure,
Proudly, I proclaim – "I am re-born –
in His Divine firmament –
a languishing victim – no more.

In His Shoes

I have been in the doorsteps of hell,
    I walked the trail, His shoes I wore,
I crossed the bridge only to return –
    not a moment too soon –
        the bridge was burned.
Gaping steel, broken span –
    all that remains of centuries' lore.

I rebuilt my home, its broken roof,
    I wore His clothes, His miner's cap,
I blew the trumpet, its muted call,
    I wore His gloves to clean the mud,
        the mask I used kept noxious gas
            and spurting blood away,
Keeping the alien dust from my broken heart.

In the bloody terrain of battles lost,
    I groped for help, I kissed the dust,
        to keep shrapnel from hitting me,
            the piercing bullet of ignominy,
The enemy's advance, I rebuffed
    my battle cry for this noble cause,
    – Heaven's listening post.
In the throes of death, in the early dawn,
    I dreamt and hoped for the setting sun,
        so darkness can cap my naked trench,
        so darkness can shroud my prison lair
            escaping once more the enemy's hand,

I knew God was with me when I cried out,
"In the valley of Death –
I fear no evil."

As the advancing shadow of mortality
knocks at my door – new vista seen,
As I swing through life, I need not be
in fear of God's infinity.

My venture unfinished, others will follow –
will wear my shoes – just as I used His.
For only when we walk the walk
share the bread with our naked hand –
and breathe gently with our heart,
can we reach God's exclusive land.

The callous, the tear, the scar, the corn
inflicted on my feet in this tenuous life
– is minuscule compared to all the pain
– which Christ endured when He came to earth.

As I freely see the twinkling star,
God's star beckoning from afar,
I know it is Jesus calling me,

As I dream of peace, my mind serene,
for I have walked his path, the rough terrain,
Faithfully, I am proud to show
His shoes I wore – my heart's aglow.

Missteps and the Superman

Missteps in life, misjudging the condition,
This is my dilemma, my past situation.
Errors I have made, sins I have committed,
Heresies I've said, my disbelieving soul,
All of these have taken their human toll —
On to the youth in me — my talents fall.

I weep, I complain — I deny the shame,
If shame does not exist, I can cry in pain,
Unhappy past I curse — others I blame,
Nowhere do you see everyone agree
That man may not be the master of his soul,
But free will with grace can yet allay the toll.

Now aged and infirmed, I have seen it all,
Lonely childhood, faulty genes those are not all,
Blaming all others for my lot in life
Means there is no world beyond for lives reborn.
I know much more than I have ever known,
There is a greater One among us all.

At 61, I must make amends,
To all whom I've hurt by my human hands,
For only in heaven — the Promised Land,
Will I find my God — my Superman.

Life Is Beautiful

   There is music in the air,
   There is music everywhere,
When I reach the peak of love and meet the dawn of life,
   There is feasting in the field,
   There is gaiety everywhere
When my fledgling soul is fused with Heaven's incantation
      – the perpetual rites of God,
There is unspeakable awe to the overdue symphony –
      the music splashing its hypnotic spell
         to a teetering humanity,
        converting despondency into Divine melody,
No more unjustified trust –
   faith at last vindicated, hope reaffirmed –
   the maternal fire once more on the roll,
   believing in each grain of sand
        that a child brings home.

Each pebble dotting the pristine sand
      glistens with the sunlight of history,
Each fallen seed from each tiny grain
      will bear again a starting plant.
The maternal voyage is on again –
     leaving not an iota of doubt
     mother - child is back on the course,
God's gentle intrusion is evident,

Eternal celebration is on hand,
Earth is illuminated by flames so dazzling –
   as they outdo the icons of mistaken lives.
Finally – music is back in the air –
There is music beyond compare
         – with the Eternal Conductor.
Indeed, life is beautiful.

Never Too Late

It is not too late to cut the cord
      to break the spell
      the game plan to revise,
It is not too late to roll with the dice
      to make another bet,
      to pull the slot,
      to choose another card.

It is not too late to disengage –
      from the force that cuts and burns,
          that derides and disrupts –
      from the razor's edge and toppling trees.
It is not too late to unmask the real culprit –
      expose false friends –
      disown egregious ways –
          and your glitzy needs.

It is not too late to say, "Hello",
      to forgive your mortal foe –
      to change your Tango steps –
      to start another play,
      to begin another cycle,
          hitting it right this time –
              from a purer base,
                  from another stage.

It is not too late to turn the clock around,
    to hit a home run,
    to pass the ball and await its return,
    the ball you will dunk as Jordan did
        – in the seismic game of life,
    – not too late to hit a lob,
    to be at par,
    to volley and run,
    to kick the goal,
and never too late to confess to ills incurred –
    to compassions withheld –
    to acknowledge debts
    and show unconditional love.

At 61 – I would like to say,
    what truly matters are the basics of life –
Games of life we all have to play –
    but it is those who hustle and get the ball,
    those who can re-invent themselves –
        who will attain the peace of the gods,
Especially if you acknowledge all –
    the greatest force of the universe –
    the Master Coach,
    the Great Planner,
    the Great Lord Jesus –
        who set us free.

Yes - it is not too late.....

No Longer in Fear

No longer do I challenge the Dogma of life,
    No longer am I haunted by the specter of the unknown,
    No longer afraid to face the naked truth,
        – to flex the muscles of human decency,
        – to stifle the dark forces of evil,
        – to enshrine virtue's best,
        – awarding the ultimate prize
            to those who have upheld the Book of Life.
No longer in fear to face the bully of life,
    No longer in fear to face the executioners' noose,
        –my pusillanimous years are passé,
No dream, however farfetched, is beyond my reach,
No goal is impossible beyond my form,
        as long as I can subdue the pessimistic force,
            and bury my negativistic stance.
My only limit is human mortality,
Human bondage, crippling miasma passé
Free at last I am from the disabling past –
    from the ungodliness and fears,
        the anxiety ridden world to which I choked,
The malevolence and the doubts
    are just footnotes in my inner chest,
        – for no longer am I in fear.
With great relief I am ready for the complex forces that loom,
    Am ready to meet the deterring forces ahead,
        the final straw to my rejuvenated self,

   the reality of my regressing physique,
For no longer am I a parolee,
  nor a lifer awaiting the final axe,
My soul, however, is so free,
  – to do my thing
    minus the pain,
    minus the timidity,
    minus my haunting doubts.

After this life – someday maybe – my progenies will read this saga,
discover with pride the jewel in me,
exalt and celebrate the star
  which beckoned my quest –
discover my Redemptive God,
  ready to accept His perfect novel,
    – its great beginning,
      and the inevitable end.
For no longer am I afraid –
Thank God, I found my peace.

Spring, Autumn, Sunset

In the spring of our lives
*   we play and flirt*
*   dive and dunk*
*   as ducklings do*
*   - in this dawn of our infancy.*
For it takes time to find ourselves
*   to define our role, our special niche*
*   in the planetary space,*
If we gracefully injure our wings
*   while pecking each others grain*
*   we can easily forgive and excuse*
*   each other's oddities*
*   the greasy seasoning of our*
*   blooming years,*
But when our roots take hold
and our branches grow
*   in the early autumn of our lives -*
We should know by then our vulnerabilities
*   - the limitation of our stars,*
Hate and doubt should leave no marks
*   Intemperance resolved -*
*   Darkness ferreted out*
*   - and all the hugging and haggling,*
*   cussing and fuming should be passé,*
Warmth and gentleness triumphant.

At the sunset of our voyage
        in this wild existence
        The past may sometimes resurface -
            regrets and remorse recycled -
        pain revived
But we need not beat ourselves
        with the rubbles of the past
No need to rummage through elusive dreams,
        the unfilled expectations of the past

Time is too precious at this dimming twilight
        all shadows must be quelled
            as another generation arrives.
        Let the gleaming light
        of our peace prevail
Let us pave the road for our grandchildren
        the newest petals of mutation
For they need to go through the same
        cycle of life
        To slip, to bloom, to peck, to glide,
Hopefully injuring less their wings
        and maintaining longer
            their ecstatic scent.

The Psalm of the Prodigal Son

I cry in your presence O' Lord –
    wailing in my tormented state,
Crossing the bar, scaling the forbidden wall –
      unlocking the safe, barging through the gate
      to no man's land –
Transgressing your Holy space,
      defying your pristine firmament,
Sprinkling doubt to the Holy Sacrament
    – my unspeakable tirade.

Numb is my heart, my soul paralyzed –
My graceless life haunted in vain by my angst –
    no honeyed words suffice –
    no contrived scheme by the human machine
      can wipe this defilement,
I have crossed the line
    – I defined the border,
    I cursed at High Heaven –
      now my pride is unraveled,
The weeping Madonna sees:
    misplaced veneration, hedonistic idols
      – man redefining humanity
    my ego trip masks my wayward youth.
Veiled attempt to usurp His throne,
    the balsamic vinegar searing His wound –
      once more re-opened at each transgression,

Steaming lava from my soul's perversion –
    my antenna to the Spirit all but past –
    gone is my youthful countenance.
Speaking in tongues is now an alien call
    when at one time I longed for this special gift.
The harshness of my ugly life has wiped all its bloom
    leaving only vile forsaken dust -
Feckless seed lay strewn in wanton disgrace
    - unwelcomed even by the decaying Earth.
As I near the end, my night lightens up
    - my sleep is finally jarred
    by the drizzling tears,
Her dazzling presence still awaiting me
    - tapping me with her royal arms,
    still with her virginal balm.

To the Royal Mother, no sinner is lost
    'till the last sigh of men's mortal breath.
In agony - I come to you O' Lord,
    - I await your call
My soul to bear the wound
    I have inflicted to all,
My soul awaits your judgment's call
    Your divine mercy I implore.

The Second Fiddle

Never the soprano, always the chorus girl,
Never the hero, always the villain,
Never the pilot, always the co-pilot,
Never the surgeon, always the assistant –
waiting for the scalpel to be handed to me,
a straight line incision, I have planned all along
– if ever given a chance to be on my own.
Never the president, always the veep
– supportive and constantly touting the presidential line,
half-heartedly joining him publicly
in his grand deception
in his disingenuous ways
Uncomfortable I may be –
political piety I have to display.

As I struggle to find myself –
I have discovered many things –
searing pain of broken lives,
gnawing stomach of homeless souls,
Hearing penance, remorseful contrition of those
who erred –
mistaken lives –
victims of unscrupulous rage –
misled creeds
touching me, stirring my human side
leaving me speechless, forgetting my private pains –
the social slur,
the political snobbery,
that has inundated my life.

As I continue to find my way,
I cannot forego the gnashing, the wailing, the weeping,
of the bereaved and the aggrieved,
"This is still earth – not yet hell," I tell myself.
But does it really matter if I am
always a second fiddle –
the second choice?
Perhaps we all need to be the alternative
at one time or another,
The trappings of my office, my life of comfort
have obstructed my view
– when only my ego, my human pride prevails –
A life of anger and angst
– understated, undermined.

But now –
Stones and knives do not hurt,
acid tongue and racial slurs cause no pain,
relegated to a lesser role, irrelevant I am –
In the eye of God – there is truly no lesser role,
no serf, no slave, no second class,
It matters not if I am a substitute,
the second or third choice,
the second or third string,

I am honored to be His Divine sidekick,
His lady in waiting –
Proud to be His Second Fiddle
in the symphony of His Holy Order.

The Saga of the Penitent

I overstayed in His Holy Land –
    the only place which welcomed me with open arms,
I sailed adrift beyond the still water –
    where He navigated the Apostles in His safety net,
I pressed the wrong button and kept pressing it –
    long after I knew it was the wrong thing to do,
I misfired the shot, the bullets entrusted to me
    – to protect lives and property,
Playing Russian roulette, taking life for granted
    as I cockily whipped my pistol with cavalier grin,
I killed the goose which laid the Golden egg
    thinking there will be bigger geese with bigger eggs,
My mind too minuscule to realize –
    that golden chances are a rarity –
    that there could be only one goose
        with the golden egg for me.

I called it quits early in the game –
    didn't persevere like my parents did –
    when faced with unrelenting obstacles
        and odious foes,
I tipped the scale, disrupting the balance
    riding high on my ego and pride,
I didn't need to put all the weight in favor of earthly needs
        ...but I did –
I put all my eggs in one basket
    – a poor choice of a basket, though,

I broke the barrier set by God –
   a wall separating the good from the bad,
My rebellion more meaningful would be –
   if I broke the contrived limbs of societal norms.
I cross the Rubicon – never glancing back –
   finalizing my onward steps –
Never looking back to wonder –
   the ominous path I have chosen –
Not wanting to know the eventual rewards
   of fidelity and sacrifice
      - if I didn't make the crossing....
I cut all the bridges behind me –
   bridges difficult to rebuild,
   – pride made me do it,
   – pride keeps me from being remorseful,
   – pride keeps me forever aloof
      never to rebuild the span
      to connect to my former land.
I pulled the lever of no return
   – pre-warned of the consequences
      ...I really didn't care,
I envisioned myself as a perpetual youth –
   with the ability to re-start at will
      – to make amends
      – to re-ignite my passion, my youthful fire,
         and triumph as always in the end.

I broke the chain that held me tight –
   no more a slave, I had the chance

to do great things, to right the wrong –
But I used my freedom to create discord –
　ignoring the basics, questioning the fundamentals –
　refusing to face the bottom line.
As my sagging body succumbs to infirmities
　– and age has crept in every strand of my
　　　dissipating flesh,
Remorseful I am for listening to the
Serpent's song –
　　　for believing I was free to do anything
　　　　which fancied me
　　　free to chart my own course with impunity
　　– believing in the "Me First" concept,
　　– believing in the concept of the Non-God
　　– believing that sin does not exist
　　　　– just men's figment and scheme.

Now – I am past the serpent's call
　that hammered on my vulnerabilities –
　　　my prurient past behind me,
I weep and wait, I bargain with Him
　– for more time to make amends,
But with the Grim Reaper in my front
　– know my time is up,
　– I beg the Lord – "Forgive,"
"Your Prodigal child is back in need – O' Lord"
　I beg of you – have mercy on my soul,
　　　　AMEN

Too Late to Matter

I came too late to fill the gap,
    the unfilled void of a troubled bud.
I came too late to mean a thing,
    – to the world he has built
    – to his fall and spring.
I came too late to the gory scene,
    the blood stained knife thrust by him,
    who was too naive to recognize –
        a snake in motion, a fox in disguise.
Too late, I arrived to impact his soul,
    too late to change his basics all,
Into my nest like a promising bird,
    he was nurtured with love so rare.
He sprouted and grew and soon came the day,
    He emerged to make the Play of the Day,
But soon dark shadows haunted his path,
    confused and troubled he became detached.
It is hard to know the twists and turns
    – of life once delightful
    – of a boy once so thoughtful.
I cannot fathom the Jekyl and Hyde
    – in each child born,
    – in each man grown,
I know now that believe I must,
    through all these hard facts, lives of misdeeds,
Not all the answers can come from men,
    if it were so, we'd understand,
I must not despair – as long as there is hope
    there will be a breakthrough in our sordid tale
    – a door which will re-open to a brighter land,
        the final peace: Heaven sent.

Rolando

He is my best friend,
        In my bosom, he will always be,
From different carriage, we each emerged
        into this contentious earth,
           - three hundred sixty five days apart -
He, from the harsh branch of a hardy tree,
          I, from the protected bloom of a perennial
        flowering plant,
But that really doesn't matter -
        for we both are cloned to a tee,
His convictions, his principles appeal to me,
    Compassion, he has in excess for the underdogs of life,
        but somehow unable to connect
           to those whose style and hymns
              are different from his.
Compulsive he is - undoubtedly,
        drops of sarcasm now and then,
Obsessive - he will always be
        - especially in a gustatory sense.
His taste is far above the rest of us -
        every speck of ingredients, he could name,
Be it a dash of MSG, sprinkled oyster sauce,
        or Rosemary glaze,
Always propelled by wine and cheese
        and savory salmon steak-
He could tell each vintage year
        of Dom Perignon and wine galore

But somehow he could never guess
        my vintage dreams, the fading vignette of my life.
He could recount an incident in microscopic detail,
        dramatize it well with teary eyes
        and choking voice,
But, oh sometimes, it could reach a boring peak,
        and sometimes each pain narrated
        reopens once more old ghastly wounds,
An anecdote many times re-told
        could incessantly jar my beleaguered ears,
        But really it is okay to me -
I understand what age can do to all of us
        - thickened fibrous strands linking wiltering cells,
        - swollen neurons, fading dendrites
        replaced by alien cells.
I, myself, need a computer to do the job
        - to recycle my stories of failed relationships
        - titillating romance
        - gyrating dreams
        - innocent camaraderie
        - misspent youth
If not - each tale would be embellished
        when details are at stake -
  making my ode more tragic
        - more enduring
        - more climactic.
O' Cruel Age - how could you so intrude
        in our dimming years,
  - indulge on our friendships

       - in our idiosyncratic ways
           - in our false nostalgia
My friend Rolando is now 63,
        - a year younger than he - I am
         and will always be
...the immutable fact which he has to accept.
But it really doesn't matter now -
      these twilight years and our waning health
         insidiously invading our vestigial sanity,
Let me look back at better times - those refining years
        in the spring of our nascent lives,
      when we were vibrant and exciting, with glossy
         dreams -
      vision propelling us to the outer space of our
         potentials,
      providing us the strength to survive
         the pain in our new found land -
    united in misery, united in our warmth
      - united with those who shared the soul's
        synergy.

Let me thank God for the good times
      - view the present as the inevitable tail end
        of this cycle of life
Let us give God his due
      in the spirit of our enduring friendship
        For always - Rolando
        Always my bosom friend -
        Semper Fideles.

No Way Out

The overcast looms ahead
    portending dark times to come,
I tremble – my fluttering heart
    – left to spur with destiny
    – left to jostle with cruel fate.

Unable to hang on my tenuous grip
    my foothold is about to give –
With one momentary snap, one false slip
    – my lifeline is gone.

Subliminal forces keep me at bay,
    O' my floundering spirit
    – my blundering heart
Unable to shake myself –
    from this goring miasma of life
    – this sordid hubris which I am entombed.

Unless I seek refuge in Him
    seek his flame of hope
"Men still have free will" so I must act
    or forsaken dust soon I will be,
He patiently awaits my call –
    this self entrapment which chokes my flesh,
Awaiting the surrender of my heart
    the final triumph of His love.

There is Still Time

There is still time
        to apply the brakes,
        to lubricate the wheels,
        to tighten the screws,
For life is like a car –
        needing wheel alignment,
        tire balancing, oil check,
        spare parts replacement.

There is still time –
        to quantify your pain,
            analyze your win,
            enjoy your net gain,
        to weld the broken pieces,
            sew the tear –
            to make amends –
            and know the difference,

There is still time –
        to stand on your feet –
            to overcome hardships –
                the travails of needless affliction,
        to curb men's sadistic
            and masochistic ways,
There is still time
        to right the wrong,
        to forgive –

   to be kind, even to those who previously
     denied your right to life,
There is ample time –
  to face the truth,
  to suture the wound,
  to undo the stark image of your past –
    to lay aside previous frivolities,
Enough time to peel the fruit,
  to scrape the skin
    when strapped to the thin bare bones
      and dangling in need.
It is only too late and too little time –
    if you refuse to face what it takes
      to recover the atoms –
      to bare the knuckles –
      to take the bull by the horn.
It is only too late –
    when you defy His loving words –
    refusing to comply with His
      Great Commandments of Life.
    and drowning to the narcotizing hold
      of the non-god.

   Then and only then
    is it too late
     to undo your life.

I "Done" It All

I swore, I cursed, I did it all,
    I pillaged my virtues with runaway vice,
I gambled, I drank, I spit with fire –
    nothing left for my hapless foes.

I danced all night – the Rock and Roll,
    risks I took – ostentatiously,
I scaled the peaks, rock climbing my glee,
    no one in this world would stand in my way.

In deep waters with impunity,
    I dived, I glided with the falls
        – daring the rapids
        – challenging the crocodile
        – wrestling the snakes and all,
I scorned the lions, I shunned the tiger,
    no men, no villain could tackle me,
        Tarzan, Saddam, Bubba, King Kong
    are not to be.

I bested the best, scorned their weaknesses,
    I drank the fire of carnal zest,
I swallowed the sword of discontent,
I sought the potion of unbridled joy,
    I imbibed the passions of the half – baked youth.

I sucked the venom – my unstoppable dreams,
    I disrupted the monastic pledge –
        entering forbidden caves,
        breaking the lock,
        undoing the knot –
    leaving loved ones in disgrace.
I pulled the plug, released the trigger,
I broke the jar, bared my body –
        exposing the fallacies of men –
            mocking their hypocritical stand.
But now at my dimming year of 61,
    I am ready to turn around –
        away from my fractious life –
If time is kind and God forgives,
        I will surrender all my worldly goods –
            rebuking my ephemeral needs
Just to live within his celestial light,
        to echo His fervent will –
            and finally share His effusive joy.

Too Soon

Too soon to know
>   the morbid side of life,
Too soon to squabble about a fire
>   that will soon be quelled,
Too soon to foresee the sad sequence
>   of a life of flaws,
Too secure to feel the pangs
>   of a deprived existence.

Too much turmoil to reveal the past –
>   afraid to instill grief and shame,
>   afraid to disrupt a life of rainbows
>   that will not last too long –
the sad entombment of the tales of men,
>   the inevitable end of fleeting joys.
Too young to know the repertoire
of the successful tenor
>   a story of persistence and will
>   adding to the genetic gift,
abstention from flighty ways –
>   the pursuit of excellence.

Too enthralled to the lure of fame and gold,
>   the narcissistic dreams for heroic acclaim
Bypassing the reality –
>   escaping responsibility.

Too soon to proclaim a final victory
    the long unfinished saga of men.
In life, there are many wins and many gains
    many losses to deny
But in actuality, it is a mix,
    the good and the bad,
    the joyous and the sad,
There is really nothing absolute and final
    in this earth,
We are all shades of black and white,
    there is no perpetual loss or permanent gain,
    it is all relative – lots of perspectives,
What matters most unquestionably,
    is how we accept the inevitable,
    and adjust the scale,
    revise the imperfect,
    recreate the scene,
    working from His basic scheme,
in so doing, we'll attain the prize
    of peace and growth,
    of joy and love –
    the satisfaction of a life well lived –
    always within His Holy Scale.
Yes – it is not too soon.

Act of Contrition

I begin the day O' Lord in praise of you,
Save me from this despondency,
Save me from my infirmities,
I have trespassed your Holy Garden,
I have transgressed your laws divine –
entering your Holy altar
unclean, unshaven, uncouth.

Let me carry your shoes, your spear, your vest,
let me reject every inch of Mammon's advances,
Put me in your dungeon of judgment –
I will warm the floor for you to tread –
I will face the spikes of your righteous wrath,
I will face the fissures and crevices of fate –
ready to fall in the churning current below
– if I so deserve,
Deserving I am of your just punishment,
Unable to undo my torrid life – now past,
– A life of trauma on hapless souls,
past victims of my hellish ire –
my lusty flesh, my wayward steps,
innocent people – maimed by my verbiage,
my darkish moods.

Save me O' Lord in my troubled life –
don't give up on me – am still your child,
I will end this day with you by my side –

    naked my soul, I cannot hide,
        – praising you, loving you for all time
Listen to my acts of contrition
        – this lifetime penitence,
Your kind mercy I beg.

Past My Prime

Past my prime
    I still can manage a contralto or two,
Past my prime
    I can lead, soaring like an eagle
        Golden spectacle of my old Air Jordan days,
Past my prime
    I still can come to the net and hit
        an unreturnable lob,
A few strokes, I still can do
        –brilliantly with a zing!
But now it does take more effort
    – drowning in sweat
    – huffing and puffing
    – with tongue wagging like Fido
        in the blazing desert of survival.
My sagging belly and pendulous waist
    flip flops at every move I make
My double chin wiggles each time I giggle,
Some complex notes still come with melodic tune
        – but I need to concentrate
Otherwise only a squeaky voice would lunge
        cheerlessly from my beaten chord.
I am called ageless – and why not!
        At 74, I still can dunk,
    But distract me not – or the ball might just enter
        the ring from below
        – if not my head in lieu,

Age and time, indeed, make obvious statements,
    But, hey, nothing much to apologize for
        Humiliated I am not –
These flaws are not mine alone
      Gaps and lapses, stuffed memories
          – like stuffed cabbages abound
Even regretting sins and errors which I have not committed,
    Nothing new– just aging,
    I am merely human, a fun-filled woman,
Once an angelic beauty, now a weathered flesh.

Consider my presence a dash, a comma –
      Past the exclamation point of my life,
Some sparks remain, here and there,
      – like flickering firefly,
A few promises unfilled,
    a few secrets untold –
        but do not brush me off –
Anything is still possible in my mind,
    The truth, however, is glaring:
        "I have gone as far as I could."
    You have seen the best of me –

Today my engine teeters,
      my motor sputters,
My battery bubbles with noxious fumes
      my tire needs retreading,

I am just gliding – merely stalling
　　　after these many years of wear and tear,
I still have some mileage left
　　but not too much.

And now another excitement awaits me,
　　　The path to the Royal road is at hand,
One time, hobnobbing with earthly kings
　　　with the world's wealthy,
Now simply trekking to Heaven's gate
　　　– pure exhilaration!
More than any part I have played
　　More than any battle fought
　The coming Celestial union
　　　is just my kind,
　True – I am past my prime
　　　– But certainly – no regrets!

God's Day - First Day of Spring

Spring has come
      cascading into my autumn life,
   Nature's beauty has dwarfed the petulance
     – the enmity within my soul,
This delightful day is here
     curbing the narrow expanse
        of my confines,
      infusing reverence to cluttered spirits
Uplifted is my tottering faith
  – the calculating grace spilling its music
to a waiting earth –

   Conjuring splendor in my downcast soul
      the cacophony of waves stirring
         my dormant dreams,
Today – I will prune the dead twigs of my past –
  Axe the tree of doubt
     and let go the negative figments –
The bad seeds are thrown away
     –no waiting soil to welcome them,
Gone is my brooding youth
    my old age angst
  In the splendor of God's day –
This magnificent spring.

It Is About Time

Resent not my wins
    – they are well deserved,
Enjoy my accolade, join my fun,
Embrace my hopes, my dreams,
    the honeyed fruit it brings,
Join the game, the balancing act
    the artful feat which I relied on,
You, too, can do it – perhaps even better,
Your prodigious talent is much more
    than I ever have.
I did it, got it right
    relying more on sweat and blood –
        wit and courage did supplement
a kindred heart, an unflinching spirit,

But –
    If you choose not to reach this level,
        – pull the lever, push the button
        – uncork the bottle
    I do understand –
        it is all right –
Not all men need to run
    or want to scrounge and scrape
        for what is left,
Some men are comfortable where they are
    For the moment
        or for perpetuity,

Some are propelled to be on the move
        from birth –
        Others feel it is their destiny to surge beyond
        barriers –
        past cosmic comforts for a higher cause –

Some need to keep swimming -
        to keep their heads above water,
        Others need to grovel
        and escape the searing flame.
But for me –
 It is a matter of survival
        – to catch the runaway dream
With grit and fidelity, my faith upholding me –
        "Though I walk through the Valley of Death –
        I fear no evil, for thou are with me."
His presence electrifies me!
        "The Lord is my Shepherd –
        no want shall I know."
Today – join me
        His blessings profuse,
        I have finally arrived,
        It is about time.

What Follows Next

After losing – what follows next?
    recriminations,
    regrets,
    restructuring,
    unloading of the losing stocks.
After the fall – what comes next?
    the fumbling and fussing,
    finger pointing,
    re-inventing,
    new projections on display.
Yet if we come to think of it –
    losing and failing is not something new –
        it is the story of life –
            its very core,
Be it Napoleon's Waterloo
    or Rome's downfall,
  What counts most
    is how you pick up the pieces
    How you get a grip of the situation,
    a new outlook,
    a creative reappraisal of what is left,
    the final resolve.

What happens next after rejection?
    downright despair,
    others derision,
    alienation from the world of the lucky ones,
    scathing criticism of your vilifying foes.

But remember –
> There is no perpetual despair –
>> unless you allow it,
> No permanent victories either –
>> just solid stocks
>>> and the incontrovertible basics of life.

If you triumph, what happens next?
> parties and celebration –
>> drinking and feasting –
> elevated self esteem,
>> cocky outlook,
> sense of immutability
>> uncalled-for infallibility,
But do not party too long –
> less you fall from your frail pedestal –
>> foundation of clay,
> egregious moves must not be displayed.

After winning the lotto, what follows next?
> smiles and laughter,
> sudden public acclaim,
> instant friendship,
> institutions knocking at your door
>> – wanting to share the dole.

When the presidency is won – what follows next?
> invitations galore,
> overnight foundations for the poor,

      high expectations,
      important pronouncements,
      contrived friendships,
      tales of escapades
          – which never occurred.

After the wedding – what follows next?
      the toasting and dancing,
      lovers saddled in mesmeric trance,
      a new world forthcoming for them,
      a benign and prodigious future
          – they hope and pray.

After the promotion – what follows next?
      a new desk for the CEO,
      embellished gold on his sculptured door,
      his word becomes gospel truth
          – for as long as he dispenses well
              and increases the NASDAQ gain.

After the Dow Jones abrupt fall – what comes next?
      "Yahoo" becomes "Boo-hoo!"
      friendly broker, now contemptuous conniver,
      morbid thoughts abound,
      guns and knives at one's disposal,
      jerky responses, sarcastic jabs.
With motherhood comes –
      reality confronting dreams,
      pounds to lose, baby-sitter to pay,

sleepless nights, crying baby,
diapers to dispose, failed breast feeding,

But be patient, do not fret
— do not give up,
for this is just transient —
they grow up fast,
once a boy — now a man.
Crying child is nothing new —
it is only our minds that are not versed
Many good things happen in life —
if we come to grips and recognize
where we are,
who we are,
where we are going.

We should never forget:
ours is an imploring and crying world,
His is a stable and solid place,
If we fall, we can always get up
— and take the cross like He did,
The victory which only counts
is from Him
— Who gave the sermon on the Mount,
Until our day is done—
and our inner fire is quelled,
Life's ironies will continue on.

For We Have Just Begun

What secret lies within your venal breast?
Where did your darkish soul come from?
What forbidden passage have you traversed?
What devilish curse has taken you –
      your petulant heart –
      your unscripted spirit,
Who intruded upon your once pristine soul?
      – igniting Heaven's wrath
      your sordid ways
      passion's spectacle,
Who injected the venomous pang of a non-God?
When did the soul and body's convergence cease?
      it's immutability in question
      by faithless travelers
      – irretrievably traumatized,
Forgiveness is given to all whose despair misleads them,
Compassion is given to all those in pain,
But Revulsion is due to any concept
      on the non-concept of the soul,
Where lies the pure and the just –
      among the lamb and the meadows green.
Heaven and the archangels see it all.
Impatient, I cry in pain,
God sees and says:
      "Await, await – the day of reckoning has not come,
      For you have just begun –
            seeing life's interplay,
      Let nature and good things flow
      Let the chirping birds with their syncopation
            lend their air, their inspiration.

      Have faith and believe –
            For we have just begun.

The Ascent -
By a Mountain Climber of Life

I am a finder –
    You are a keeper,
        I have visions – you stifle them,
My zeal – you disdain –
    favoring the comfort of the secure
        – preferring the safety net of the
            middle ground.

Frozen in fear –
    An onlooker you'd rather be
        – than a rescuer of souls,
Preferring neutrality than to face the task
    – to reverse the unspeakable
    – the odious abortion of rights
    – the ignominious plight of the deprived.

For me –
    No deterring gutsy wind
        can dislodge my resolve,
On perfidious mountain cliff –
    I have found my foothold
Clutching tightly the craggy rocks
    overlooking the abysmal depth –
    While my body rests astride
        on treacherous terrain
            teetering from my tenuous hold.

I know
    The harness may give way
        but I believe in this ascent
    With bloody grasp, I will overcome
        the ridges and fissures of life,
    My spirit is lodged secure
        in the power of this noble flight,
    I will reach the mountain peak
        and set the anchor tight –
    For I believe in this ascent
        in the crescendo of my climb
        in the **faith** that empowers me
            – the Omnipotent by my side.

Let the Day Begin

Let the day begin with the rivers and oceans of wonder,
Let the day begin with the fallen leaves
reattached to their stem –
like homeless children reunited with their parents.

Let the day begin with the roar of a moral earthquake
crushing men's malevolence –
effacing the malice which has seeped his soul.
Let the day begin with the peaks and valleys,
cracks and fissures of humanity
leveled into a plane of tolerance and temperance.
Let the day begin preparing for the night
when tiny little stars band together
to outshine and outlast the brazen sun.

Let the day begin with the untouchable coming down to earth
and the unfathomable brought to simplicity.
Let the day begin with the righteous man
prevailing against a tepid world.
Let the day begin conjuring splendor
from the mud and hut of rickety lives.
Let the day begin with fallen angels
dethroned from space –
His anger assuaged.

Let the day end –
in His wonder and justice,
in His kindness and mercy,

For only then is the cycle of life complete –
the beginning and end of life is one,
day and night fused,
the soul and body synergized.
"Dust thou art to dust returnest"
is truly spoken from the soul.